Greta L. Singer

ALICIA E. PORTUONDO

GRETA L. SINGER

SPANISH
FOR
SOCIAL WORKERS

(Senda didáctica)

SENDA NUEVA DE EDICIONES
New York
1981

ACKNOWLEDGMENT

We want to express our gratitude to the Grant-in-Aid Committee of Monmouth College, West Long Branch, New Jersey for the grant that helped to make this book possible. We are also grateful to our students who, by using the manuscript in class, have encouraged us to publish it.

Copyright © 1981 by Alicia E. Portuondo and Greta L. Singer
Senda Nueva de Ediciones, Inc.
P. O. Box 488
Montclair, N. J. 07042

ISBN: 0-918454-25-5
Library of Congress Catalog Card Number: 80-53983
Printed in the United States of America

All rights reserved. No part of this publication covered by the copyright hereon may be reproduced or used in any form or by any means—graphic, electronic or mechanical, including photocopying, recording, taping, or information and retrieval systems—without written permission.

SPANISH
FOR
SOCIAL WORKERS

OBRAS PUBLICADAS POR SENDA NUEVA DE EDICIONES

I. SENDA BIBLIOGRAFICA

Elio Alba-Buffill y Francisco E. Feito. *Indice de El Pensamiento [Cuba, 1879-1880].*
Alberto Gutiérrez de la Solana. *Investigación y crítica literaria y lingüística cubana.*

II. SENDA NARRATIVA

Oscar Gómez Vidal. *¿Sabes la noticia...? ¡Dios llega mañana!* (cuentos)
Ignacio R. M. Galbis. *Trece relatos sombríos.* (cuentos)
José Vilasuso. *El día de la liberación.* (cuentos)
Alberto Guigou. *Días ácratas. Sin ley ni Dios.* (novela)

III. SENDA DE ESTUDIOS Y ENSAYOS

Octavio de la Suarée, Jr. *La obra literaria de Regino E. Boti.*
Rose S. Minc. *Lo fantástico y lo real en la narrativa de Juan Rulfo y Guadalupe Dueñas.*
Elio Alba-Buffill. *Los estudios cervantinos de Enrique José Varona.*
Rose S. Minc., Editor. *The Contemporary Latin American Short Story [Symposium].*
Rosa Valdés-Cruz. *De las jarchas a la poesía negra.*
Ada Ortuzar-Young. *Tres representaciones literarias en la vida política cubana.*
Suzanne Valle-Killeen. *The Satiric Perpective: A Structural Analysis of Late Medieval, Early Renaissance Satiric Treatises.*
Festschrift José Cid-Pérez. Editores: Alberto Gutiérrez de la Solana and Elio Alba Buffill.
Ignacio R. M. Galbis. *De Mío Cid a Alfonso Reyes. Perspectivas críticas.*
Angela M. Aguirre. *Vida y crítica literaria de Enrique Piñeyro.*

IV. SENDA POETICA

Lourdes Gil. *Neumas.*
Gustavo Cardelle. *Reflejos sobre la nieve.*
Xavier Urpí. *Instantes violados.*
Esther Utrera. *Mensaje en luces.*
Eugenio Florit. *Versos pequeños* (1938-1975).
Frank Rivera. *Construcciones.*
Marjorie Agosin. *Conchalí.*

V. SENDA ANTOLOGICA

Alberto Gutiérrez de la Solana. *Rubén Darío: Prosa y Poesía.*
Roberto Gutiérrez Laboy. *Puerto Rico: Tema y motivo en la poesía hispánica.*

VI. SENDA LEXICOGRAFICA

Adela Alcantud. *Diccionario bilingüe de psicología.*

VII. SENDA DIDACTICA

Alicia E. Portuondo y Greta L. Singer. *Spanish for Social Workers.*

PREFACE

Conversation is our primary method of communication. Basic communication among two or more persons follows no set pattern. it is a relaxed exchange of thoughts and feelings. In a more controlled conversation, certain ideas can be highlighted; goods or services can be bought or sold; information can be conveyed or elicited. When the latter technique is more structured, and the skill more refined, a conversation can become an interview.

A purposeful interview is the result of knowledge, study and practice. It is based on a thorough understanding of human behavior and motivation. It can become a finely honed tool for use in the social worker—client relationship. This relationship can be enhanced by a sense of rapport between interviewer and interviewee. Rapport, however, is hampered by a lack of communication when both parties do no share the same language.

This book was written to help the English speaking social worker overcome the language barrier without the necessity of formal Spanish lessons. We have included chapters based upon sample interviews, in both languages, each slanted toward a particular social problem. We have used specific phrases necessary to assist the social worker in eliciting proper information from the client. We have added a comprehensive vocabulary, and a section dealing with the pronunciation of the language.

We then realized that our book could be an invaluable aid for other client contacts within any agency. With this end in mind, we have devoted our first chapter to a basic review of interviewing skills. This chapter may serve to bolster flagging self-confidence, be used as a handy review, or help a paraprofessional put a client at ease. Regardless of your particular need for this review, we hope it will help you to help your client. Helping others is what our profession is all about.

Good luck.

Alicia E. Portuondo

Greta L. Singer

INTRODUCTION

The first interview in a worker-client situation is crucial. It is the product of years of study. It is a time to put into use the principles and techniques we have learned. It is a time to blend the life experiences we have gathered from our backgrounds and personal relationships with scientific knowledge. This blending of knowledge, practical experience, and common sense gradually increases and rounds out our interviewing skills. Thus, we make the transition from beginner to experienced interviewer.

The attitudes of an interviewer are predicated on motivation, prejudices and tolerance. These are the very same bases that motivate our clients. It is necessary for us to realize that the behavior resulting from such motivation may be unconscious as well as conscious. There are, also, subjective and objective aspects to each situation which require careful evaluation. Such evaluation will enable the interviewer to understand the rationalizations clients often use to cover up painful issues. The interviewer is then better able to understand the interviewee's underlying motives and feelings, and listen for clues as to the actual focus of the interview.

We tend to believe that prejudice is only concerned with color and class distinctions. We fail to realize how more subtle prejudices can affect our relationship with our clients. Do we over respond to clients we like? Are we more sympathetic toward one family member in preference to another? Are we able to tolerate shortcomings in our clients? Are we aware of the positive and negative sides in a relationship? We must not ignore the feelings these questions raise. Awareness of our possible reactions to these issues enables us to control our attitudes.

Some of us arrive at decisions more quickly than others. However, we are all subject to conflicting ideas and emotions. It is important not to allow these conflicts to interfere in arriving at a proper decision. Generalizations, judgments and rigid classifications should always be avoided. It is much more important to seek an understanding of behavior than it is to condemn it. Understanding generates tolerance, and this leads to acceptance of the interviewee's feelings.

Interviewing skills and problem solving are interrelated throughout counseling. It is vital for us to realize that we do not begin by looking for the ultimate solution. A goal is only achieved by a series of steps, where-in one solves one small problem at a time. An important first step is to obtain an understanding of the client's problem. Then we must decide whether the agency is equipped to assist the client in this area. If services are not available through this agency, referral to another agency should be made. This must be explained to the client and all necessary assistance given. In the case of referrals, ask the client to phone you to let you know if it was successful. You must be certain that no further action on the part of your agency is necessary before the case can be closed.

Thorough understanding is based on listening. Permit the client to present the problem without interrupting. Specific questions should be asked later. A good worker is always interested in the client's manner of speaking while presenting the problem. Tensions, excitement, and hesitations all help the interviewer understand the complete picture. A few nods, smiles, ahas, etc., will serve to assure the client you are listening.

The first few minutes of an interview are well spent in making the client feel at ease. Try to arrange for someone to take your calls, and eliminate all other interruptions. This sets the scene for a relaxed atmosphere, and contributes to the feeling of confidentiality. This is a vital element in a successful interview.

Greetings, introductions, and some short preliminary phrases (in the language the client is most comfortable with) help set the tone of the interview. This is the time for the interviewer to offer basic information about smoking or rest room facilities. The following example offers some carefully selected statements to initiate the first interview. It further illustrates the format of our bilingual section of the text. Opening the interview with a few pleasantries gives the client an opportunity to relax prior to presenting the problem. This particular sample is on a very elementary level. Many of the questions could easily be handled by a paraprofessional or receptionist.

Good morning.	Buenos días.
I am a social worker at ———.	Soy un trabajador social en ———.
Please — Sit down. Make yourself comfortable.	Siéntese. Póngase cómodo.
May I help you?	¿Puedo ayudarlo?

Successful interviewing techniques should avoid the use of tricky questions. It is preferable to phrase questions that cannot be answered by simple «yes» or «no» answers. Allow the client to set the pace of the interview. Above all, this is not the time for role playing on your part. You are neither a detective seeking hidden motives, nor a psychiatrist attempting to probe the **unconscious**.

Common Concerns of Interviewers

Conventions differ as to the use of first names, and the setting of the interview is a major influence in arriving at a proper decision. It is usually recommended that last names be used in an office. This helps to emphasize the professional rather than the social nature of the relationship. It also shows respect for the adult client who, because of the need to ask for assistance, may feel cast in an inferior role. It is never correct to ask adult clients to address the worker by the last name if the worker fails to exted the same courtesy.

The beginning worker is concerned with maintaining the formality of the interview, so personal questions and comments posed by the client can create a problem. Brief, frank, and truthful answers to personal questions are best in most instances. It is also helpful to ascertain the reasoning behind a particular question. The client may not understand something, or may be concerned about the worker's qualifications or experience. If the interviewer is aware of the concern that prompts the question, the reply can usually be dealt with briefly and reassuringly.

Frequently a client comes to an agency with a spouse, children, or an entire family group. It is best to ask the spokesperson whether the interview is to be conducted in private or with the accompanying persons. If the family unit remains, it is most important to observe the interaction among the members. It is especially important for the worker to follow culturally acceptable behavior e.g., with an hispanic family always be sure to speak to the husband first. Ask for his opinion and suggest that he check with his wife. Traditionally the man assumes the lead role and may resent it if you speak to other family members without his consent.

If the client comes with a friend or neighbor, you may want to suggest that the non-family member wait in the waiting room. The client may be too shy to suggest this, but be most willing to follow your lead. This would ensure greater privacy and confidentiality between the client and yourself.

Remember to begin «where the client is». Sort out the most pressing concern and explain further actions which are necessary in order to help ease the problem. It is wise to ask the client to restate your summary or instructions to make sure you were heard and understood correctly. Always be specific about details and see that important addresses, phone numbers, and names of persons to be contacted **are given to the client in writing.**

Encourage the client to contact you if other problems arise before the next appointment, and see that the client receives an appointment card. The client should understand that you are to be notified if the appointment cannot be kept. You should also assure the client that you will do the same in the event that you are unable to keep the appointment.

PRONUNCIATION

The Spanish language is easy to pronounce based on the fact that letters will *always* have the same sound, regardless of their position in a word. This makes a refreshing change from English.

There are 30 letters in Spanish; they are divided into vowels and consonants.

There are five vowels; they are:
- a   is similar to the English a in cat: p*a*-dre, c*a*-s*a*
- e   is similar to the e in send: m*e*-sa
- i   is similar to the i in machine: s*i*-lla
- o   is similar to the o in bone: c*o*n-de
- u   is similar to the English oo in pool: m*u*-cha-cho

There are twenty-five consonants, they are:
- b and v,   which are pronounced alike, and sound like a weak English b: *b*-oca, *v*a-so
- c   is pronounced in Spanish America like the English s in send: c*e*-der, when written before e or i. In other cases, c is pronounced with an explosive sound, like the c in coin: *c*a-sa
- ch   is pronounced like in English: mu-*ch*a-*ch*o
- d   has two sounds. At the beginning of a word group or after l or n, it is pronounced like a weak English d. In other positions, it is pronounced like the soft English th in thought: *d*e-*d*o, ca-*d*a
- f   is pronounced like in English: *F*e-li-pe
- g   before e and i sounds like an exaggerated English h: Jor-*g*e, co-*gí*. In other positions, g sounds like a weak English g: *g*ra-cias
- h   is always silent: *h*a-blo
- j   is pronounced like the Spanish g in the combinations ge and gi: ba-*j*o
- k   is similar to English: *k*i-ló-me-tro
- l   is pronounced like in the English word lead: *l*e-ga*l*
- ll   is similar to the y in yes: *ll*e-vo
- m   is similar to English: *m*a-dre
- n   is similar to English: *N*i-co-lás
- ñ   is like ny in English: ni-*ñ*o

13

p is similar to the English p: *P*e-dro
q is similar to the English k: *q*ue-so, *q*uin-to. (It is always followed by an unpronounced u.)
r has two sounds. At the beginning of a word, or after l, n, or s, it sounds like when the tongue strikes in succession the upper teeth: *R*o-ber-to, *r*o-bo. In other positions, the tongue strikes the upper teeth with a single tap: pe-*r*o.
rr never begins a word. The sound is more prolonged than in the r: Pe-*rr*o
s is like s in the English word send: ca-*s*a
t is similar to the English t, but without aspiration: *t*o-do
w is a foreign letter, and is pronounced as in English: *W*agner
x is pronounced in two ways. Before a consonant, it is pronounced like s in send: e*x*-te-rior. Before vowels, it is pronounced like gs: e-*x*a-men.
y is pronounced like the English y in you: *y*o, tu-*y*a
z is pronounced in Latin America like the English s in send: *z*a-pa-to

All letters in Spanish are single; therefore, *ch* will be found in a dictionary after the *c*, as an independent letter.

The correct Spanish pronunciation can be easily obtained by means of the following rules of *word stress*:
1. Words that end in a vowel, or in the consonants n or s, are stressed in the next to the last syllable: *Car-men, ca-sa, pe-rros.*
2. Words that end in a consonant, except n or s, are stressed in the last syllable: pa-*pel*
3. Any word in violation of the above two rules will have a written accent (ʹ): pa *pá,* e-*xá*-me-nes

The written accent will also be written on top of vowels in words pronounced alike in order to differentiate their meaning: sí (yes), si(if). It will also be placed on interrogative words: ¿cómo? (how), ¿cuándo? (when).

A correct normal speed in pronunciation will be obtained by means of these *linking rules*:
1. A final vowel and the initial vowel of the next word are pronounced in one syllable: libro azul
2. Words that end in a consonant are linked with the next word if it begins with a vowel: el examen

Punctuation:
An inverted question mark *(¿)* is placed at the beginning of a question. The regular question mark is placed at the end of the question. The same happens with the exclamation point, that an inverted point *(¡)* is placed before the exclamation: ¿dónde estás? (where are you?), ¡qué bonita! (how pretty!). A comma is not placed between the last two words of a series: Ella usa vestido, cartera y sombrero.

In Spanish only the first word in a sentence and proper names are capitalized.

GRAMMAR NOTES

Gender of nouns
They are masculine or feminine:
1. Most masculine nouns end in *o*, el libro
2. Most feminine nouns end in *a,* la casa
3. Regardless of ending, nouns denoting male beings are masculine, female beings are feminine: la mujer, el hombre

Plurals
If a noun ends in:
1. vowel (except i, adds *s:* las casas
2. consonant (except *s)* also in í, y, add *es (z* changes to *ces):* la luz, las luces
3. plural masculine includes both genders: los hijos, the sons or sons and daughters.

Definite articles
The English definite article has only one form (the). In Spanish there are four forms wih agrement in gender and number with the noun.

	singular	plural
masculine	el	los
feminine	la	las

el libro, los libros
la casa, las casas

Indefinite articles
English has two indefinite articles: *a* and *an*. In Spanish there are four with agreement in gender and number with the noun.

	singular	plural
masculine	un	unos
feminine	una	unas

The plural means: a few, some, any ie. a few persons = unas personas

The English you
Spanish has four translations for *you* (subject pronoun)

Tú	used when speaking to close friends, children and members of your own family.
Usted	(abbreviated Ud.) used when speaking to a person one does not know very well. It needs the third person singular of the verb. You must use this form when you speak to your client.
Vosotros -as	used in Spain when speaking to a group of people one knows very well. In Latin America it is replaced by *ustedes*.
Ustedes	(abbreviated Uds.) used when speaking to a group of people one does not know very well. Use this form when you speak to two or more clients.

WORKER - CLIENT

INTRODUCTION

Good morning
Good afternoon
Good evening
My name is ⸺
I am a social worker at (state name of your agency).

I will try to help you.
Please feel free to ask me about anything you do not understand.
Please come into my office.
Sit down. Make yourself comfortable.
Yes, smoking is permitted.
No, smoking is not permitted.
Let the children play here while we talk.

REST ROOMS
Would you like to use the rest room? the water fountain?
Would your children like to use the rest room? the water fountain?

TRABAJADOR SOCIAL - CLIENTE

INTRODUCCION

Buenos días
Buenas tardes
Buenas noches
Mi nombre es ⸺.
Soy un trabajador social en (indique el nombre de su agencia).

Trataré de ayudarle.
No tema preguntar cualquier cosa que no comprenda.

Venga a mi oficina, por favor.
Siéntese. Póngase cómodo.

Sí, se puede fumar.
No, no se puede fumar.
Deje que los niños jueguen aquí mientras hablamos.

SERVICIOS
¿Quiere usar el baño? la fuente de agua

¿Quieren usar sus niños el baño? la fuente de agua?

TALKING ABOUT THE PROBLEM

I am handling your case now.

If it is approved, it will be transferred to the Under Care Unit.

If your case is not approved, you have the right to request a fair hearing.

The agency will verify the information you submit.

Please tell me your name.
How do you spell it?
May I have your address?
Your previous address?
Do you have a different postal address than your residence?
Do you pay for living with your family or friends?
May I have your telephone number?
What is your marital status?
Your social security number
Name of husband/wife
Does he/she have the same address as you?
Names and ages of children
Are the children living with you?
If not, may I have their address?
The school and grade of each child who lives with you

HABLANDO SOBRE EL PROBLEMA

Yo estoy ocupándome de su caso.

Si es aprobado, será remitido a la Unidad Bajo Cuidado.

Si su caso no es aprobado, Ud. tiene derecho de pedir revisión.

La agencia verificará la información que Ud. está presentando.

Dígame su nombre, por favor.
¿Cómo lo deletrea?
¿Cuál es su dirección?
¿Su dirección anterior?
¿Tiene Ud. una dirección postal diferente a su residencia?
¿Le cobran a Ud. por vivir con familiares o amigos?
¿Cuál es su número de teléfono?
¿Cuál es su estado civil?
El número de su seguro social
Nombre del esposo/esposa
¿Tiene él/ella la misma dirección que Ud.?
Nombre y edad de los niños
¿Están los niños viviendo con Ud.?
Si no, ¿puedo tener su dirección?
Escuela y grado de cada niño que vive con Ud.

Do you pay for care for any child under six years old?	¿Paga Ud. por el cuidado de alguno de sus hijos menores de seis años?
Name, address, phone, and amount paid to the babysitter	Nombre, dirección, teléfono y cantidad que paga a su niñera
How long is your child taken care of? Hours and days?	¿Cuánto tiempo le cuida a su hijo? ¿Horas y días?
What other relatives live with you?	¿Qué otros familiares viven con Ud.?
When and where were you born? (The same question is to be used for all people living in the same household.)	¿Dónde y cuándo nació Ud.? (La misma pregunta será usada con todas las personas que vivan en la misma dirección.)
Are you a United States citizen?	¿Es Ud. ciudadano de los Estados Unidos?
Are you a veteran of the Armed Forces?	¿Es Ud. veterano de las Fuerzas Armadas?
Do you receive veteran's pension?	¿Recibe Ud. pensión de veterano?
If you are a foreigner: date of entrance to the U.S. show that you are a legally approved foreigner	Si Ud. es extranjero: fecha de entrada en los EE.UU. (Estados Unidos) demuestre que Ud. es residente legal
Did you get married outside the U.S.?	¿Se casó fuera de los EE.UU.?
Are you separated without legal order? (divorced)	¿Está Ud. separada sin orden legal? (divorciada)
If divorced: date court where it took place	Si Ud. está divorciada: fecha corte donde sucedió
Are your parents alive? Age, please.	¿Viven sus padres? La edad, por favor.

Have you studied or trained for a special field?

Do you have other skills or hobbies which may help?

¿Ha estudiado o recibido entrenamiento para algún campo de especialización?

¿Tiene Ud. otras habilidades o aficiones que puedan ayudarle?

FINANCIAL

Are you presently employed?

What is your gross income?

Expenses of work (transportation, uniforms, union, etc.)

Name and address of your employer

Is your spouse presently employed?

What are the sources of the family income?

Do you study?
    Where?
    Hours?
    What type of study?

Do you get:
    child support?
    a pension
    social security?
    disability?
    unemployment?
    welfare?
    food stamps?

ESTADO ECONOMICO

¿Está Ud. empleado en este momento?

¿Cuánto es su salario en bruto?

Gastos del trabajo (transporte, uniformes, gremio, etc.)

Nombre y dirección del patrono

¿Está su esposo empleado en este momento?

¿Cuáles son las fuentes de ingreso de su familia?

¿Estudia Ud.?
    ¿Dónde?
    ¿Horas?
    ¿Qué clase de estudios?

¿Recibe Ud.:
    mantenimiento del niño?
    alguna pensión?
    seguridad social?
    incapacidad?
    desempleo?
    asistencia social?
    cupones de alimentos?

Medicaid?	asistencia médica: Medicaid?
Medicare?	asistencia médica· Medicare?

Do you have:
  medical insurance?
  Blue Cross?
  Blue Shield?
  Major Medical?
	¿Tiene Ud.:
	  seguro médico?
	  Blue Cross?
	  Blue Shield?
	  Major Medical?

How much premium do you pay for medical insurance?	¿Cuánto paga por las primas de ese plan médico?
Do you have any union benefits?	¿Tiene Ud. beneficios de algún sindicato de trabajadores?

Do you have any bank accounts?
  savings
  checking
  other
	¿Tiene Ud. cuenta en algún banco?
	  de ahorro?
	  de cheques?
	  otra clase?

What are your savings?	¿Cuáles son sus ahorros?
Do you receive additional help from anyone? Explain.	¿Recibe Ud. ayuda económica de alguien? Explique.
Do you want financial help?	¿Quiere Ud. ayuda económica?
Have you received assistance before?	¿Ha recibido asistencia antes?
When was the last time?	¿Cuándo fue la última vez?
How much?	¿Cuánto?
What place?	¿En qué lugar?
Why did you stop receiving it?	¿Por qué dejó de recibirla?
How much did you receive?	¿Qué cantidad recibía?
Did you receive food stamps?	¿Recibía cupones de alimentos?

How have you been supporting yourself until now?	¿Cómo se ha mantenido hasta ahora?
Do you own stocks or bonds?	¿Tiene Ud. acciones o bonos?
Do you have life insurance?	¿Tiene Ud. seguro de vida?
Under who's name?	¿A nombre de quien?
Did you pay income taxes last year?	¿Pagó Ud. impuestos de ingreso el año pasado?
Before receiving help you must go to the legal department, so you can declare if your husband helps you or not.	Antes de recibir ayuda tiene que ir al departamento legal, para que declare si su esposo la ayuda o no.
Do you want us to refer you for welfare?	¿Quiere Ud. que lo remitamos a la ayuda social?
Do you wish to receive food stamps?	¿Desea recibir cupones de alimentos?
If your children (those for whom you are asking assistance) are older than six years old, you are required to enroll in the WIN program.	Si sus hijos (por los que pide ayuda) son mayores de seis años, Ud. tiene que inscribirse en WIN.

HOUSING / VIVIENDA

Are you renting an apartment or house?	¿Vive Ud. en un apartamento o casa alquilada?
Do you have a lease?	¿Tiene Ud. un contrato de arrendamiento?
For how long is the lease?	¿Por cuánto tiempo es su contrato de arrendamiento?
Do you have any problems with your house?	¿Tiene Ud. problemas con la vivienda?

Do you pay:
  electricity?
  telephone?
  gas?
  water?
  trash pick up?
  other?
	¿Paga Ud.:
	  electricidad?
	  teléfono?
	  gas?
	  agua?
	  recogida de basura?
	  otros?

Are you looking for housing?	¿Está Ud. buscando una vivienda?
How many rooms are you looking for?	¿De cuántas habitaciones es la vivienda que está Ud. buscando?
In what neighborhood (town, city, municipality, etc.) are you looking?	¿En qué barrio (pueblo, cuidad, municipio, etc.) está Ud. buscando?
Why are you looking?	¿Por qué está Ud. buscando?
How soon must you move?	¿Cuándo debe Ud. mudarse?
Have you been evicted?	¿Ha sido Ud. desalojado?
How much rent are you paying now?	¿Qué alquiler está Ud. pagando ahora?

Have you contacted:
  a real estate agent?
	¿Ha visto Ud.:
	  a un agente de bienes raíces?

the housing office at the Welfare Department?	la oficina de viviendas en el Departamento de Bienestar Social?
the local housing authority?	la oficina de viviendas local?
Do you want us to refer you for assistance for housing?	¿Quiere Ud. que lo refiera para obtener ayuda para la vivienda?
Do you own or are you buying a house	¿Es dueño Ud. de una casa, o está comprando una casa?
Where is it located?	¿Dónde está situada?
Do you have a mortgage?	¿Tiene Ud. una hipoteca?
Is there a lien on the house?	¿Tiene su casa algún embargo?

Do you receive any profit?

Have you sold any property lately?

How much did you receive for for the sale?

Can you pay your mortgage?

Are you behind in your payments?

Have you paid your property taxes?

Does your place need repair?
   window
   basement
   electrical wiring
   walls
   ceiling
   floors
   furnace - heat
   roof
   stopped up sink
   bathroom plumbing

¿Recibe Ud. ingresos de la casa?

¿Ha vendido Ud. alguna propiedad últimamente?

¿Cuánto recibió por la venta?

¿Puede Ud. pagar su hipoteca?

¿Está Ud. atrasado en sus pagos?

¿Ha pagado Ud. sus impuestos sobre la vivienda?

¿Necesita arreglos su casa?
   ventana
   sótano
   cables eléctricos
   paredes
   cielo raso
   pisos
   calefacción
   techo
   lavamanos tupido
   tuberías del baño

PAYMENT OF UTILITIES

Do you have heat or are you cold?

What kind of heat?
   gas
   oil
   electric

Are you behind in your payments?

PAGO A LAS EMPRESAS DE SERVICIO PUBLICO

¿Tiene Ud. calefacción o pasa frío?

¿Qué clase de calefacción?
   gas
   petróleo
   eléctrica

¿Está Ud. atrasado en sus pagos?

Do you have:
    electric light?
    water?
    hot water?

¿Tiene Ud.:
    luz eléctrica?
    agua?
    agua caliente?

SANITARY CONDITIONS

Has the Health Department contacted you?

Have you any dogs or cats?
    How Many?
Are you plagued by:
    roaches?
    mice?
    bed bugs?
    lice?
Has your landlord provided an exterminator?

CONDICIONES SANITARIAS

¿Ha sido Ud. visitado por el Departamento de Sanidad?

¿Tiene Ud. algún perro o gato?
    ¿Cuántos?
¿Hay en su casa:
    cucarachas?
    ratones?
    chinches?
    piojos?
¿Le ha provisto el dueño los servicios de un exterminador de insectos?

TRANSPORTATION

Do you own a car?
Do you have a driver's license?

Does anyone in your family have a:
    car?
    driver's license?

TRANSPORTE

¿Tiene Ud. un carro?
¿Tiene Ud. licencia para manejar?

¿Tiene algún miembro de su familia:
    un carro?
    licencia para manejar?

Do any of your relatives, friends, or neighbors have a car?	¿Tiene alguien en su familia, amigos o vecinos un carro?
Would they be willing to drive you?	¿Podrían ellos llevarlo?
Do you live near a bus, subway, train, or senior citizens transports?	¿Vive Ud. cerca de una parada de ómnibus, subterráneo o metro, tren, o transporte para personas de edad?

MEDICAL CARE

CUIDADO MEDICO

Do you have a family doctor?	¿Tiene Ud. un médico para la familia?
Do you have a doctor for the children?	¿Tiene Ud. un médico para los niños?
Do you have a dentist?	¿Tiene Ud. un dentista?
Do you have a gynecologist?	¿Tiene Ud. un ginecólogo?
Do you go to the clinic?	¿Va Ud. a la clínica?
Which clinic?	¿Qué clínica?
Do you go to the hospital?	¿Va Ud. al hospital?
Which hospital?	¿Qué hospital?
For what problem?	¿Para qué problema?
How often do you go?	¿Con qué frequencia va Ud.?
For how long have you been going?	¿Por cuánto tiempo ha estado Ud. visitándolo?
Do you have a nurse that visits you at your home?	¿Tiene Ud. una enfermera que lo visite en su casa?
Are you taking medication?	¿Toma Ud. medicinas?
Do you know the name of the medication?	¿Sabe Ud. el nombre de la medicina?
Do you need your medication refilled?	¿Necesita Ud. más de estas medicinas?

Do you have the money to do this?
Do you have a drug store?
Do you need glasses?
Do you have an optometrist?
Do you need a hearing aid

¿Tiene Ud. dinero para comprarlas?
¿Tiene Ud. una farmacia?
¿Necesita Ud. espejuelos?
¿Tiene Ud. un optometrista?

GENERAL HEALTH

Are you in good health?
Are the members of your family in good health?
Do you have:
    high blood pressure?
    low blood pressure?
    diabetes?
    heart disease?
    ulcer?
    stroke?
    anemia?
    headache?
    allergy?
    emphesyma?
    backahe?
    stomach ache?
    fever?
    nervousness - «bad nerves»?
    loss of appetite or weight?

loss of sleep - insomnia?
    pains?
    glaucoma?
    morning sickness?
    Are you pregnant?

SALUD EN GENERAL

¿Tiene Ud. buena salud?
¿Tienen los miembros de su familia buena salud?
¿Tiene Ud.:
    presión alta?
    presión baja?
    diabetes?
    problemas cardíacos?
    úlcera?
    embolia?
    anemia?
    dolor de cabeza?
    alergia?
    enfisema?
    dolor de espaldas?
    dolor de estómago?
    fiebre?
    nerviosismo?

    pérdida de apetito o peso?
falta de sueño - insomnio?
    dolores?
    glaucoma?
    malestar por la mañana?
    ¿Está Ud. embarazada?

When do you expect the baby?

Will you need assistance for the baby?

Do you want me to refer you for health care?

¿Cuándo espera que nazca su bebé?

¿Necesitará ayuda para su bebé?

¿Quiere Ud. que lo refiera para que obtenga asistencia para la salud?

CHILD CARE PROBLEMS

PROBLEMAS DEL CUIDADO DEL NIÑO

Are your children attending school?
What is the name of the school?

What grade is your child in?
What is the teacher's name?

What is the principal's name?

Is your child having any problems in school?
Does your child speak English?
Does your child have learning problems in:
  Math?
  English?
  Physical Education?
  Social Studies?

  Reading?
Does your child have problems with other children?
  fighting
  name-calling

¿Están sus niños asistiendo a la escuela?
¿Cuál es el nombre de la escuela?
¿En qué grado está su niño?
¿Cuál es el nombre del maestro?
¿Cuál es el nombre del director de la escuela?
¿Tiene su niño problemas en la escuela?
¿Habla inglés su niño?
¿Tiene su niño problemas en:

  matemáticas?
  inglés?
  educación física?
  estudios sociales?
  historia?
  lectura?
¿Tiene su niño problemas con otros niños?
  peleas
  se insultan

shyness	timidez
Does your child have difficulty sitting still?	¿Tiene problemas su niño para sentarse derecho?
Do you have money for school lunches?	¿Tiene Ud. dinero para los almuerzos en la escuela?
Is your child in school:	¿Está su niño en la escuela:
all day?	todo el día?
half a day?	medio día?
mornings?	por la mañana?
afternoons?	por la tarde?
Do you need someone to watch your children when you go to:	¿Necesita a alguien que cuide a sus niños cuando Ud. va:
the hospital?	al hospital?
the clinic?	a la clínica?
work?	al trabajo?
shopping?	de compras?
Do you want your child (children) to attend a:	¿Quiere Ud. que su niño (sus niños) asista(n) a:
day care center?	un centro de cuidado diario?
nursery school?	nursery school?
kindergarten?	kindergarten?
Do you want to send your children to camp this summer?	¿Quiere Ud. enviar este verano a sus niños a un campamento de verano?
overnight	para dormir allí
day camp	por el día solamente
neighborhood recreation program	al programa recreacional del barrio
Do you have money to pay?	¿Tiene Ud. dinero para pagarlo?
Do you need a scholarship?	¿Necesita una beca?
Do you have money for clothing for your child?	¿Tiene Ud. dinero para comprarle ropa a su niño?
Does your child have all the required inoculations?	¿Tiene su niño todas las vacunas requeridas?

Is your child in good health?
Are you happy?

¿Tiene su niño buena salud?
¿Está Ud. contento?

PARENT-CHILD PROBLEMS

PROBLEMAS DE LOS PADRES E HIJOS

Please note that for some of these questions you may substitute other members of the family, such as:

husband	esposo
niece	sobrina
nephew	sobrino
brother	hermano
sister	hermana
son	hijo
daughter	hija

Does your child obey you?
¿Lo obedece su hijo?

Is your child staying out at night?
¿Se queda su hijo fuera de la casa por la noche?

Is your child missing school without your permission or without your knowledge?
¿Falta su hijo a la escuela sin su permiso o sin su conocimiento?

Do you believe that your son/daughter is:
  drinking alcohol?
  smoking marijuana?
  taking drugs?

¿Cree Ud. que su hijo/hija está:
  tomando alcohol?
  fumando marijuana?
  usando drogas?

Is your son having problems with any member of the household?
¿Tiene su hijo problemas con algún miembro de la casa?

Is the school complaining about your child?
¿Se queja la escuela de su hijo?

Do you like your son's friends?
¿Le gustan los amigos de su hijo?

DELINQUENCY OR LAW ENFORCEMENT PROBLEMS

Have the police been in touch with you about your child?
Has your child ever been arrested?
Are there any charges against your child now?
Has your child been to the juvenile conference committee?
Has your child been to juvenile court?
Is your child on probation?

Is your child on parole?

What is the probation officer's name?

Do you need legal services?

What is the name of your lawyer?
What is his phone number?

May I phone him?
Is your son in:
    the juvenile shelter?

    county home of detention?
    county jail?
    reformatory?
    state prison?
    federal prison?
What help do you need?

DELINCUENCIA O PROBLEMAS EN EL CUMPLIMIENTO DE LA LEY

¿Le ha llamado la policía por causa de su hijo?
¿Ha sido arrestado su hijo?

¿Está su hijo acusado ahora?

¿Ha estado su hijo en la conferencia del comité juvenil?
¿Ha estado su hijo en la corte de menores?
¿Está su hijo bajo libertad provisional?
¿Está su hijo en libertad bajo palabra?
¿Cuál es el nombre del agente encargado de la libertad provisional?
¿Necesita Ud. servicios legales?
¿Cuál es el nombre de su abogado?
¿Cuál es el número de teléfono de su abogado?
¿Puedo llamarlo?
¿Está su hijo en:
    el albergue para menores?
    el vivac del condado?
    cárcel del condado?
    reformatorio?
    prisión del estado?
    prisión federal?
¿Qué ayuda necesita?

Do you want me to refer you to:
   a lawyer?
   legal aid?
   probation department?

parole department?

¿Quiere Ud. que lo refiera a:
   un abogado?
   ayuda legal?
   departamento de libertad provisional?
   departamento de libertad bajo palabra?

MARITAL PROBLEMS / PROBLEMAS CONYUGALES

Please note: substitutions for the word spouse are:

boyfriend	amigo
girlfriend	amiga
lover	amante
husband	esposo
wife	esposa
man	hombre
woman	mujer

Are you separated from your husband?
¿Está Ud. separada de su esposo?

When did your spouse leave?
¿Cuándo la dejó su esposo?

Have you been deserted?
¿Ha sido Ud. abandonada?

Do you know where your spouse is?
¿Sabe Ud. dónde está su esposo?

Does your spouse give you money?
¿Le da dinero su esposo?

Does your spouse show violent behavior?
¿Tiene su esposo un carácter violento?

Does he beat you?
¿Le pega él?

Does he beat your children?
¿Les pega a sus niños?

Does he break things around the house?
¿Rompe él cosas en la casa?

Have you filed charges against your spouse?	¿Ha presentado Ud. cargos contra su esposo?
Do you think your spouse would be willing to come here?	¿Cree Ud. que su esposo estaría dispuesto a venir aquí?
with you?	con Ud.?
alone?	solo?
Does your husband know you are here?	¿Sabe su esposo que Ud. está aquí?
Do you expect to tell him?	¿Piensa decírselo?
Are you contemplating divorce?	¿Piensa divorciarse?
Are you contemplating a short separation?	¿Piensa Ud. separarse por un corto tiempo?
Are you contemplating a long term separation?	¿Piensa Ud. separarse por un largo tiempo?
Have you ever been for counseling?	¿Ha buscado Ud. consejos antes?
Where, when, and for how long?	¿Dónde, cuándo y por qué tiempo?
Does your spouse speak English?	¿Habla inglés su cónyuge?
Is your spouse having problems with the children?	¿Tiene su cónyuge problemas con los niños?
Is your spouse having problems with other members of the household?	¿Tiene su cónyuge problemas con otros miembros de la casa?
Would you like to be refered for marriage counseling?	¿Le gustaría que la refiriéramos a un consejero matrimonial?
Does your husband take your welfare check?	¿Le coge su esposo su cheque de bienestar social?
Does he take your food stamps?	¿Le coge él sus cupones de alimentos?
for alcohol	para tomar bebidas?
to pay debts	para pagar deudas?

EXTENDED FAMILY

Do any of your relatives live with you?
  mother
  father
  aunt
  uncle
  cousin
  grandchildren
  niece
  grand niece
  nephew
  grand nephew
  grandfather
  grandmother

How is your relationship with him (her, them)?
How long has this relationship lasted?
Do you support him/her (them)?
Does he/she (they) need any help?
  old age assistance
  medical care
  housing
Is your elderly relative depressed?
Is your relative senile?
Has he/she problems remembering things?
Is your relative lonely?

Is he/she adjusting to being in this country?

OTROS MIEMBROS DE LA FAMILIA

¿Viven con Ud. algunos parientes?
  madre
  padre
  tía
  tío
  primo(-a)
  nietos
  sobrina
  sobrina nieta
  sobrino
  sobrina nieta
  abuelo
  abuela

¿Cómo se lleva Ud. con él (ella, ellos, ellas)?
¿Desde cuándo existe esta relación?
¿Lo/la (los, las) mantiene Ud.?
¿Necesita (n) él/ella (ellos, ellas) alguna ayuda?
  asistencia para los ancianos
  ayuda médica
  ayuda con la vivienda
¿Está deprimido su pariente anciano?
¿Está senil su pariente?
¿Tiene él/ella dificultad en recordar cosas?
¿Se siente solitario su pariente?
¿Se ajusta él/ella a estar en este país?

Does your relative have his own income?   ¿Tiene su pariente ingresos propios?
Is your relative able to help in [with] the work at home?   ¿Puede ayudar su pariente en el trabajo de la casa?
Do you need nursing care for your relative in a nursing home?   ¿Necesita que le cuiden a su pariente en un hogar de ancianos?
Do you need to get «Meals on Wheels» for your relative?   ¿Necesita Ud. servicio de alimentos a domicilio para su pariente?
Do you need day care for your relative while you work?   ¿Necesita que cuiden a su pariente mientras Ud. trabaja?
Do you need clothing for your relative?   ¿Necesita Ud. ropa para su pariente?
Do you need medication for your relative?   ¿Necesita medicinas para su pariente?
    a doctor?   un médico?
    a nurse in your home?   una enfermera en su hogar?
    hospital care?   cuidado en el hospital?
    glasses?   espejuelos?
    special appliances, such as: aparatos especiales, tales como;
    walker   andador
    hospital bed   cama de hospital
    cane   bastón
    wheelchair   silla de ruedas
Would you like me to give you the address of a senior citizens club?   ¿Quiere que le dé la dirección de un club de ancianos?
Do you have any other problems with this relative?   ¿Tiene Ud. otros problemas con este pariente?
Do you know your priest? [pastor?]   ¿Conoce Ud. a su sacerdote?
Do you belong to a church group?   ¿Pertenece Ud. a un grupo religioso?
What is the name of the priest? [pastor?]   ¿Cuál es el nombre del sacerdote?

Do you belong to a church
May I phone him?

Has the church given you any assistance?

Do you want the priest to visit your elderly relative?

¿Pertenece Ud a una Iglesia?
¿Puedo llamarlo por teléfono?

¿Le ha dado la iglesia alguna ayuda?

¿Quiere que el sacerdote visite a su pariente anciano?

REFERRAL FOR SERVICE

This is the name of the agency that can help you.

This is the address.

This is the phone number.

This is how you get there.

Do you want me to phone them to make an appointment for you?

What day and time would be good for you?

You will need to bring the following information with you.
    Receipts of bills:
        rent
        gas
        electric
        oil
        water
        telephone

DIRECCIONES PARA OBTENER SERVICIO

Este es el nombre de la agencia que puede ayudarle.

Esta es la dirección.

Este es el número de teléfono.

Esta es la forma de llegar allá.

¿Quiere Ud. que los llame para hacerle una cita?

¿Qué día y a qué hora le convendría?

Usted necesitará traer consigo la siguiente información.
    Recibos de cuentas:
        del alquiler
        del gas
        de electricidad
        de petróleo
        de agua
        de teléfono

mortgage	de la hipoteca
medical	de médicos
child care	de cuidado del niño
transportation	de transportación
doctors' reports	reportes médicos
marriage certificate	certificado de matrimonio
birth certificate	certificado de nacimiento
baptism certificate	certificado de bautismo
Would you like a social worker of this agency to interview you about any of the following matters?:	¿Desea Ud. que un trabajador social de esta agencia lo entreviste además sobre alguno de estos asuntos?:
training in order to find a job	entrenamiento para buscar trabajo
look for a job now	buscar ahora empleo
education	educación
legal services	servicios legales
budgeting	formas de distribuir sus ingresos
family planning	planeamiento familiar
problems with your children	problemas con los hijos
difficulties regarding housing (problems with the landlord)	dificultades relacionadas con su vivienda (problemas con el dueño)
doctors, dentists, child care	médicos, dentistas, cuidado de los hijos
other problems	otros problemas

DIRECTIONS ON HOW TO GET TO THE AGENCY

The name of the agency is ———————.

The address is ———————.

You can take the bus at the corner of ——————— and get off at ———————.

You can get a taxi at the corner of ———————.

Do you want me to phone a taxi?

You can walk to the agency.

Turn left (right) and go straight for ——————— blocks.

Do you want me to phone the agency and make an appointment for you?

Do you want me to phone the agency and tell them you are on the way?

What day and time do you want for your next appointment?

I would like to see you again.

May I visit you at your home?

How do I get to your home?

What day and time would be best for you?

Do you want me to phone you before I come?

I will phone you when I have the information you want.

DIRECCIONES SOBRE COMO LLEGAR A LA AGENCIA

El nombre de la agencia es ———————.

La dirección es ———————.

Usted puede tomar el autobús en la esquina ——————— y bajarse en ———————.

Usted puede tomar un taxi en la esquina ———————.

¿Quiere que le llame un taxi?

Usted puede caminar a la agencia.

Doble a la izquierda (derecha) y vaya derecho por ——————— cuadras.

¿Quiere que llame por teléfono a la agencia y le haga una cita?

¿Quiere que llame a la agencia y le diga que Ud. está en camino?

¿Qué día y hora prefiere para su próxima cita?

Me gustaría verlo otra vez.

¿Puedo visitarlo en su casa?

¿Cómo llego a su casa?

¿Qué día y hora sería mejor para Ud.?

¿Quiere que lo llame por teléfono antes de venir?

Le llamaré cuando tenga la información que quiere.

I will write to you when I have the information you need.

Please phone me or come in again if you need more help.

Le escribiré cuando tenga la información que Ud. necesita.

Por favor, llámeme o venga otra vez si necesita más ayuda.

AGENCY FORMS

FORMULARIOS DE LA AGENCIA

We have included some samples of agency forms on the following pages. They may help you to familiarize yourself with official forms.

Please complete forms carefully and answer all questions accurately.

Some questions are required for statistical purposes only. You will not affect your eligibility by answering.

Do you understand our official forms?

Do not sign any form before you read it. If you are in doubt about anything on the form, please ask for help.

Hemos incluido algunos modelos de formularios en las páginas siguientes. Ellos le ayudarán a familiarizarse con los formularios oficiales.

Por favor, complete el formulario con cuidado y las preguntas con exactitud.

Algunas preguntas son necesarias sólo por razones estadísticas. Usted no afecta su eligibilidad al contestar.

¿Comprende nuestros formularios oficiales?

No firme ningún formulario antes de leerlo. Si Ud. tiene dudas sobre algo del formulario, por favor, pida ayuda.

SUMMER DAY CAMP
CAMPAMENTO DIURNO DE VERANO

NAME
_____
NOMBRE

ADDRESS——————————   TELEPHONE——————
DIRECCION   TELEFONO

AGE   DATE OF BIRTH   GRADE
_____   _____   _____
EDAD   FECHA DE NACIMIENTO   GRADO

+ NOTE: IF MORE THAN ONE CHILD IN THE FAMILY QUALIFIES TO PARTICIPATE IN THE CAMP, PLEASE FILL OUT THE BOTTOM PART OF THIS APPLICATION.

+ NOTA: SI MÁS DE UNO DE SUS NIÑOS CUALIFICA PARA PARTICIPAR EN EL CAMPAMENTO DE VERANO, FAVOR DE LLENAR LA PARTE BAJA DE ESTA APLICACION.

NAME	AGE	BIRTH DATE	GRADE
NOMBRE	EDAD	FECHA DE NACIMIENTO	GRADO
_____	____	_____	_____
_____	____	_____	_____
_____	____	_____	_____
_____	____	_____	_____
_____	____	_____	_____

_____
PARENT OR GUARDIAN SIGNATURE
FIRMA DEL PADRE O ENCARGADO

HEALTH FORM FOR SUMMER DAY CAMP

FORMULARIO DE SALUD PARA EL CAMPAMENTO DIURNO DE VERANO

Name————————————————————————
Nombre

Address————————————————Telephone——————
Dirección   Teléfono

Age——————— Date of Birth————Parent's Name———
Edad   Fecha de nacimiento Nombre de padre o
                                    madre

Whom to contact in case of emergency————————————
                        Name and relationship to the child
A quien notificar en caso de emergencia
                        Nombre y relación con el niño

————————————————————————
                              Address and telephone
                              Dirección y teléfono

Is your child on medication? Yes———No———
If yes, please explain————————————————
¿Está tomando su hijo medicamentos? Sí———No———
Si es sí, favor de explicar—————————————

Does your child have any physical or mental problems that would prevent him from participating in some of the camp's activities? Yes——No—— Explain:————————————

¿Tiene su niño algún impedimento físico o mental que le impida participar en algunas de las actividades del campamento? Sí——No—— Explique:————————————

Is your child allergic to any type of medication? Yes——No——
If so, name them:————————————
¿Es su hijo alérgico a algún tipo de medicamento? Sí——No——
Si es sí, cuales son:————————————

Is your child allergic to anything else besides medication? (ex. bee stings, flowers, certain kinds of fruits, animals, etc.) Yes——No——
Explain:————————————

¿Es su hijo alérgico a alguna otra cosa aparte de medicamento? (ej. picadas de abejas, flores, algunas frutas, animales, etc.) Sí——No——
Explique:————————————

In case of an emergency will you allow that your child be taken to the hospital's emergency room and be treated by the physician on duty? Yes——No—— If no, whom do we contact?

En caso de emergencia, ¿nos permitirá Ud. que llevemos a su niño a la sala de emergencia del hospital y que sea tratado por el médico en turno Sí——No—— Si no, ¿con quién nos ponemos en contacto?

————————————————
Name
Nombre

————————————————
Address and telephone
Dirección y teléfono

State

~~Please put~~ your identification number for any hospitalization plan you have.

Por favor, escriba su número de identificación de cualquier plan de hospitalización que tenga.

_____

Medicaid   Blue Shield/Blue Cross   Other
                                                  Otro

_____

Date   Parent or Guardian Signature
Fecha   Firma del padre o encargado

_____ **RETURN TO** _____

(Regional Office Address)

APPLICATION TO PROVIDE FOSTER CARE

Male Applicant——————— Female Applicant———————
              (name)   (name—include
                                                         maiden name

Address———————————————————————
    (number)   (street)   (city)   (state)   )zip code)

County———————Home Phone (include area code)———

Office Phone(include area code)——————— ———————
                (male applicant)   (female applicant)

	Male Applicant	Female Applicant
Birthdate		
Religious Affiliation		
Race		
U.S. Citizen (Yes or No)		
If Naturalized: Date and Place		
Marriage: Date and Place		
Present Occupation		
Name and Address of Employer		
Social Security Number		

Age, sex and number of children desired ————————————

Have you ever had a foster child before? ( ) No ( ) Yes

If so, from ———————————— to ————————————

If so, from what agency or individual was the child received? ————

Names of your Child(ren)	Sex	Birthdate	School Grade or Occupation	Address (if child not living at home)

Names of Others Living in your Home	Sex	Age	School Grade or Occupation	Relationship to you

As part of the foster parenting study process, every member of your household will be required to have a physical examination.

NAME AND ADDRESS OF PHYSICIAN:

    Male Applicant ——————————————————————
    Female Applicant ————————————————————
    Children ——————————————————————————

In the interests of all concerned, we routinely run a police check. Arrests and/or convictions will not automatically disqualify anyone from our foster parenting program.

Have you or any member of your family ever been arrested and/or convicted of a crime? ( ) No ( ) Yes

If so, please explain: ─────────────────────────
──────────────────────────────────────

Persons (not related) whom we may contact as references concerning you as an individual and as a potential foster parent:

Name	Address	Telephone (include area code)

Directions for reaching your house by automobile (after reaching your town):

──────────────────────────────────────

──────────────────────────────────────

──────────────────────────────────────

─────────────────────   ─────────────────────
Signature of Male Applicant   Signature of Female Applicant

─────────────────────
Date Signed

DEVUELVA A

(Dirección oficina de distrito)

SOLICITUD PARA OBTENER HIJOS DE CRIANZA
(FOSTER CARE)

El solicitante ―――――――― La solicitante ――――――――
            (nombre   (nombre - incluya el apellido
                                                                                  de soltera)

Dirección ――――――――――――――――――――――――
      (número)   (calle)   (ciudad)   (estado)   (zona postal)

Condado ――――――― Teléfono del hogar (incluya el área) ―――

Teléfono de la oficina (incluya el área ―――――― ―――
                        (el solicitante)   (la solicitante)

	El solicitante	La solicitante
Fecha de nacimiento		
Religión		
Raza		
Ciudadano de E.E.U.U. (sí o no)		
Si naturalizado: fecha y lugar		
Fecha y lugar de matrimonio		
Ocupación actual		
Nombre y dirección del empleador		
Número del Seguro Social		

Edad, sexo y número de hijos de crianza que desea ——————

¿Han cuidado Uds. alguna vez a un hijo de crianza? ( ) No ( ) Sí

Si lo tuvieron, desde —————— a ——————

Si lo tuvieron, ¿de qué agencia o individuo lo recibió? ——————

Nombres de su(s) hijo(s)	Sexo	Fecha de nacimiento	Grado en la escuela u ocupación	Dirección (si su hijo no vive en el hogar)

Nombres de otros que viven en el hogar	Sexo	Edad	Grado en la escuela u ocupación	Relación con Ud.

Como parte del proceso para convertirse en padres de crianza, cada miembro de su hogar tendrá que tener un examen médico.

NOMBRE Y DIRECCION DEL MEDICO:

El solicitante ——————————————————
La solicitante ——————————————————
Hijos ——————————————————————

Para beneficio de todos los interesados, habitualmente hacemos una prueba policial. Arrestos y/o condenas no descualifican a nadie automáticamente de nuestro programa de padres de crianza.

¿Ha sido Ud. o algún miembro de su familia arrestado y/o declarado culpable de un crimen? ( ) No ( ) Sí

Si es sí, favor de explicar: ─────────────────
────────────────────────────────

Personas (que no sean parientes) con quienes podemos ponernos en contacto, que puedan dar informes de Ud. como individuo y padre de crianza potencial:

Nombre	Dirección	Teléfono (incluya el área)

Como llegar a su casa por automóvil (después de llegar a su pueblo):
────────────────────────────────
────────────────────────────────
────────────────────────────────

───────────────── ─────────────────
FIRMA DEL SOLICITANTE   FIRMA DE LA SOLICITANTE

─────────────────
FECHA EN QUE SE FIRMA

AGREEMENT

between

THE AGENCY

and

FOSTER BOARDING PARENTS

The agency approves your home as a foster home for children. In order to avoid misunderstanding, the following agreement is drawn up to clarify the respective responsibilities of the agency and the foster boarding parents:

The agency will assist you in carrying out your responsibility toward the child by giving you information regarding the child's needs through suggestions and consultation regarding care of the child;

The social worker will visit your home and the child regularly, and will be available to give any service needed for the child's welfare;

The agency will pay board to boarding parents, for each child placed in your home, at the current rate;

The agency will provide each child with a basic wardrobe upon placement as required and will send quarterly clothing allowances to boarding parents for replacements in an amount in accordance with each child's age and sex;

The agency will be responsible for arranging and paying for necessary medical and dental care and treatment for the child placed in your home when informed that the child is in need of such care and treatment;

The agency will be responsible for arranging overall plans and visiting plans for the child's parents and for helping to keep the child informed about the situation of his own family;

The agency will share with you plans for removal of the child from your home as soon as this information is available and will share responsibility for helping to prepare the child for the change.

We, the foster boarding parents, agree as follows:

We will be responsible for providing the child with a normal wholesome home life, including adequate shelter, well-balanced diet, affection, understanding, development of self-responsibility, training, recreation, education, moral and ethical training, appropriate religious guidance if the child has a faith, and opportunity for social relations with other children and adults;

We will give the worker information regarding the child and his development, will consult with the social worker before making important decisions, and will permit the worker to have individual conferences with the child;

We agree that we shall not make independent plans for the child's welfare with his parents, relatives, or others and that we shall not receive money or other payments for the child's care except with the knowledge of the agency;

We understand that the child will retain his own legal name to which he has a right;

We will arrange for the child to see his own parents or relatives in private according to a plan worked out with the agency;

We secure consent from the agency before taking the child for extended visits or vacations outside of the city or county;

We will notify the agency immediately if the child develops abnormal behavior;

We will notify the agency immediately of illness of the child or of any serious illness of any members of our family;

We will arrange for emergency medical care for the child in accordance with the plan previously set up for each child and within policies of the agency;

We will notify the agency of any change in our address or any change in the membership of our family;

We will incur no expenditure without authorization from the agency if reimbursement is expected;

If, for any reason, we cannot keep the child or properly care for him, we will immediately notify the agency and give the agency time to make other plans for the child and to prepare him for the change;

We will board no child except those approved by the agency;

We will assist in preparing the child for leaving our home so that he can comfortably move on, regardless of our personal feeling about future plans for him.

FOSTER CARE AGREEMENT

between

PARENT(S) OR LEGAL GUARDIAN

and

THE AGENCY

I hereby request the agency to place my child(ren) ——————
————————————————————————————————
in a foster care or a group setting. I understand I am not surrendering my parental rights.

In requesting placement of my child(ren), I understand that the agency will assume responsibility for my child(ren) in accordance with the provisions of the agency.

In addition, I authorize the agency to provide and consent to any operation, treatment or diagnostic test for my child(ren) which may be advised by the attending physician or dentist, provided that in case of serious illnesses or major operations I shall be notified whenever possible.

I will agree to keep the agency informed at all times of any change in my address and to cooperate in planning for the best interests of my child(ren). It is understood that visits with my child(ren) will be arranged through the caseworker at such time as may be agreed upon by the agency, the foster parents, and me. While my child(ren) is in placement, I will discuss with the agency all future plans for him.

I understand that the agency will advise me concerning my child(ren)'s progress, except that I grant permission to the agency to make such plans as may be necessary in an emergency when I cannot be reached.

Mother ———————————   ———————————
    (full signature)   (address

Father ———————————   ———————————
    (full signature)   (address)

Legal Guardian ——————   ———————————
    (full signature)   (address)

                                                                         ———————————
                                                                           (date signed)

———————————————   ———————————
(signature of Social Worker)   (district office address)

                                                                         ———————————
                                                                           (telephone no.)

ACUERDO

entre

LA AGENCIA

y

LOS PADRES DE CRIANZA

La agencia aprueba su casa como hogar de crianza para niños. Para evitar malos entendidos, el siguiente convenio se ha establecido para aclarar las respectivas responsabilidades de la agencia y de los padres de crianza.

La agencia le ayudará a cumplir sus responsabilidades hacia el niño dándole información sobre sus necesidades a través de consultas y sugerencias.

El trabajador social visitará su casa y al niño regularmente y estará disponible para dar cualquier servicio necesario para el cuidado del niño.

La agencia pagará la comida de cada niño a los padres de crianza al precio corriente.

La agencia proveerá a cada niño al ser colocado, la ropa básica y dará cuotas trimestrales para reponerla de acuerdo con las necesidades de edad y sexo.

La agencia será responsable de dar y pagar por tratamiento médico o dental de cada niño situado en su casa cada vez que dicho tratamiento sea necesario.

La agencia será responsable de tomar medidas y planes de visita de los padres naturales y mantener a los niños informados de la situación en su propia familia.

La agencia compartirá con Ud. los planes para mudar al niño de su casa tan pronto como esta información esté disponible, y compartirá también la responsabilidad de preparar al niño para el cambio.

Nosotros, los padres de crianza, convenimos lo siguiente:

Seremos responsables de dar al niño un hogar normal y sano, incluyendo cama, una bien balanceada dieta, cariño, entendimiento, sentido de responsabilidad, entrenamiento, recreación, educación, estímulo moral y ético, guía religiosa si el niño tiene alguna fé y oportunidad de relaciones sociales con otros niños y adultos.

Daremos al trabajador información sobre el niño y su desarrollo; consultaremos con él antes de hacer decisiones importantes, y permitiremos conferencias individuales con el niño.

Convenimos que no se harán planes independientes para el bienestar de niño con sus padres, parientes u otros, y no aceptaremos dinero u otros pagos para el cuidado del niño excepto con el consentimiento de la agencia.

Entendemos también que el niño conservará su nombre legítimo al cual tiene derecho.

Haremos los arreglos necesarios para que el niño vea a sus padres naturales o parientes en privado y con previo plan con la agencia.

Conseguiremos permiso de la agencia antes de sacar al niño en visitas o vacaciones extensas fuera de la ciudad o condado.

Notificaremos inmediatamente a la oficina del distrito si el niño desarrolla conducta anormal.

Notificaremos inmediatamente a la oficina del distrito si el niño se enferma o si ocurre alguna enfermedad seria a cualquier miembro de la familia.

Haremos los arreglos necesarios para dar asistencia médica de emergencia al niño de acuerdo con previo plan establecido para cada niño dentro de las normas vigentes de la agencia.

Notificaremos a la oficina del distrito de cualquier cambio en nuestra dirección o cualquier cambio en el número de miembros en nuestra familia.

No incurriremos en deudas sin la autorización de la agencia si se espera reembolso.

Si por alguna razón no podemos cuidar del niño como se debe, inmediatamente notificaremos a la oficina del distrito y daremos a la agencia tiempo para tomar otras medidas y preparar al niño para el cambio.

No daremos pupilaje a ningún niño sin la aprobación de la agencia.

Ayudaremos a preparar al niño a salir de nuestra casa de manera que pueda mudarse con toda comodidad, sin importar cualquier sentimiento personal que tengamos en cuanto a los planes futuros del mismo.

_____   _____   _____
(firma del supervisor)   (oficina del distrito)   (fecha)

_____   _____
(firma del padre de crianza)   (firma de la madre de crianza)

_____   _____
(dirección, ciudad y condado)   (fecha)

ACUERDO DE CUIDADO TEMPORERO

entre

LOS PADRES NATURALES O GUARDIAN LEGAL

y

LA AGENCIA

Por este medio doy mi consentimiento a la agencia para colocar mis hijos ——————————————————————————
en casa de crianza o en cuidado en grupo. Entiendo que bajo ningún concepto estoy renunciando a mis derechos de padre (o madre).

Al consentir que me coloquen a mis hijos, entiendo que la agencia asumirá la responsabilidad de ellos de acuerdo con las reglas de la agencia.

Autorizo a la agencia a proveer y permitir cualquier operación, tratamiento o examen diagnóstico a mis hijos siempre y cuando esté prescrito por el doctor o dentista que los atiende; y con la condición de que seré avisado, cuando sea posible, en caso de enfermedad grave o de operación de cuidado.

Convengo también en informar a la agencia cualquier cambio de dirección y cooperar en los planes que beneficien los mejores intereses de mis hijos. Se sobreentiende que las visitas a mis hijos serán concertadas a través del trabajador social cuando la agencia, los padres de crianza y yo así lo dispongamos. Mientras mis hijos estén colocados en casas ajenas discutiré todos los planes futuros con la agencia.

Entiendo que la agencia me informará con respecto al progreso de mis hijos con la excepción de que le permito a la agencia tomar las medidas necesarias en caso de emergencia cuando yo no esté accesible.

Madre ─────────────   ──────────────────
       (firma completa)   (dirección)

Padre ─────────────   ──────────────────
       (firma completa)   (dirección)

                              ──────────────────
                                  (fecha de firma)

──────────────────────   ──────────────────────
(firma del trabajador(a) social)   (dirección de la oficina del distrito)

                              ──────────────────
                                     (teléfono)

SPANISH VERBS AND SUBJECT PRONOUNS

The infinitive of a Spanish verb consists of a stem (habl) and an ending (-ar). The three conjugations in Spanish end in -ar, -er, -ir, and are usually referred to as the first, second, and third conjugations, respectively.

To form the present tense of regular verbs of the first conjugation, add the endings -o, -as, -a, -amos, -áis, -an to the stem of the verb.

hablar, to speak

SINGULAR

(yo)	hablo	I speak, do speak, am speaking
(tú)	hablas (fam.)	you speak, do speak, are speaking
(él)	habla	he speaks, does speak, is speaking
(ella)	habla	she speaks, does speak, is speaking
usted	habla (polite)	you speak, do speak, are speaking

PLURAL

(nosotros)	hablamos	we speak, do speak, are speaking
(nosotras)	hablamos	we (f.) speak, do speak, are speaking
(vosotros)	habláis (fam.)	you speak, do speak, are speaking
(vosotras)	habláis (fam.)	you (f.) speak, do speak, are speaking
(ellos)	hablan	they speak, do speak, are speaking
(ellas)	hablan	they (f.) speak, do speak, are speaking
ustedes	hablan (fam. and polite)	you (pl. speak, do speak, are speaking

The present indicative endings of -er verbs (second conjugation) are: -o, -es, -e, -emos, -éis, -en. Remember that the present tense is translated: como, I eat, do eat, am eating.

comer, to eat

SINGULAR		PLURAL	
como	I eat	comemos	we eat
comes	you (fam.) eat	coméis	you (fam.) eat
come	he, she, it eats	comen	they eat
Ud. come	you (polite) eat	Uds. comen	you eat

The present indicative endings of -ir verbs (third conjugation) are: -o, -es, -e, -imos, -ís, -en. These endings are the same as those for -er verbs, except in the first and second persons plural. The present tense is translated: vivo, I live, do live, am living.

vivir, to live

SINGULAR		PLURAL	
vivo	I live	vivimos	we live
vives	you (fam.) live	vivís	you (fam.) live
vive	he, she, it lives	viven	they live
Ud. vive	you (polite) live	Uds. viven	you live

REGULAR VERBS

THE SIMPLE TENSES

INFINITIVE

hablar to speak   comer to eat   vivir to live

PRESENT PARTICIPLE

hablando speaking   comiendo eating   viviendo living

INDICATIVE MOOD

PRESENT

I speak (do speak, am speaking), etc.	I eat (do eat, am eating), etc.	I live (do live, am living), etc.
hablo	como	vivo
hablas	comes	vives
habla	come	vive
hablamos	comemos	vivimos
habláis	coméis	vivís
hablan	comen	viven

IMPERFECT

I was speaking (used to /would/ speak, spoke), etc.	I was eating (used to /would/ eat, ate), etc.	I was living (used to /would/ live, lived), etc.
hablaba	comía	vivía
hablabas	comías	vivías
hablaba	comía	vivía
hablábamos	comíamos	vivíamos
hablabais	comíais	vivíais
hablaban	comían	vivían

PRETERIT

I spoke (did speak), etc.	I ate (did eat), etc.	I lived (did live), etc.
hablé	comí	viví
hablaste	comiste	viviste
habló	comió	vivió
hablamos	comimos	vivimos
hablasteis	comisteis	vivisteis
hablaron	comieron	vivieron

FUTURE

I shall (will) speak, etc.	I shall (will) eat, etc.	I shall (will) live, etc.
hablaré	comeré	viviré
hablarás	comerás	vivirás
hablará	comerá	vivirá
hablaremos	comeremos	viviremos
hablaréis	comeréis	viviréis
hablarán	comerán	vivirán

CONDITIONAL

I should (would) speak, etc.	I should (would) eat, etc.	I should (would) live, etc.
hablaría	comería	viviría
hablarías	comerías	vivirías
hablaría	comería	viviría
hablaríamos	comeríamos	viviríamos
hablaríais	comeríais	viviríais
hablarían	comerían	vivirían

SUBJUNCTIVE MOOD

PRESENT

(that I may speak, etc	(that) I may eat, etc.	(that) I may live, etc.
hable	coma	viva
hables	comas	vivas
hable	coma	viva
hablemos	comamos	vivamos
habléis	comáis	viváis
hablen	coman	vivan

-ra PAST

(that) I might speak, etc.	(that) I might eat, etc.	(that I might live, etc.
hablara	comiera	viviera
hablaras	comieras	vivieras
hablara	comiera	viviera
habláramos	comiéramos	viviéramos
hablarais	comierais	vivierais
hablaran	comieran	vivieran

IRREGULAR VERBS

Infinitive	Imperative	Present Indic.	Imperfect	Past
dar	dé Ud.	doy	daba	di
to give		das		diste
		da		dio
		damos		dimos
		dais		disteis
		dan		dieron
decir	diga Ud.	digo	decía	dije
to say		dices		dijiste
		dice		dijo
		decimos		dijimos
		decís		dijisteis
		dicen		dijeron
estar	esté Ud	estoy	estaba	estuve
to be		estás		estuviste
		está		estuvo
		estamos		estuvimos
		estáis		estuvisteis
		están		estuvieron
haber		he	había	hube
to have		has		hubiste
		ha		hubo
		hemos		hubimos
		habéis		hubisteis
		han		hubieron
hacer	haga Ud.	hago	hacía	hice
to do, make		haces		hiciste
		hace		hizo
		hacemos		hicimos
		hacéis		hicisteis
		hacen		hicieron

ir to go	vaya Ud.	voy vas va vamos vais van	iba ibas iba íbamos ibais iban	fui fuiste fue fuimos fuisteis fueron
oír to hear	oiga Ud.	oigo oyes oye oímos oís oyen	oía	oí oíste oyó oímos oísteis oyeron
poder to be able	pueda Ud.	puedo puedes puede podemos podéis pueden	podía	pude pudiste pudo pudimos pudisteis pudieron
poner to put	ponga Ud.	pongo pones pone ponemos ponéis ponen	ponía	puse pusiste puso pusimos pusisteis pusieron
querer to wish	quiera Ud.	quiero quieres quiere queremos queréis quieren	quería	quise quisiste quiso quisimos quisisteis quisieron
saber to know	sepa Ud.	sé sabes sabe sabemos sabéis saben	sabía	supe supiste supo supimos supisteis supieron
salir to go out	salga Ud.	salgo sales sale salimos salís salen	salía	salí saliste salió salimos salisteis salieron

ser to be	sea Ud.	soy eres es somos sois son	era eras era éramos erais eran	fui fuiste fue fuimos fuisteis fueron
tener to have	tenga Ud.	tengo tienes tiene tenemos tenéis tienen	tenía	tuve tuviste tuvo tuvimos tuvisteis tuvieron
traer to bring	traiga Ud.	traigo traes trae traemos traéis traen	traía	traje trajiste trajo trajimos trajisteis trajeron
venir to come	venga Ud.	vengo vienes viene venimos venís vienen	venía	vine viniste vino vinimos vinisteis vinieron
ver to see	vea Ud.	veo ves ve vemos veis ven	veía veías veía veíamos veíais veían	vi viste vio vimos visteis vieron

CARDINAL NUMBERS

un(o), una	one
dos	two
tres	three
cuatro	four
cinco	five
seis	six
siete	seven
ocho	eight
nueve	nine
diez	ten
once	eleven
doce	twelve
trece	thirteen
catorce	fourteen
quince	fifteen
dieciséis	sixteen
diecisiete	seventeen
dieciocho	eighteen
diecinueve	nineteen
veinte	twenty
veintiuno(a)	twenty-one
veintidós	twenty-two
veintitrés	twenty-three
veinticuatro	twenty-four
veinticinco	twenty-five
veintiséis	twenty-six
veintisiete	twenty-seven
veintiocho	twenty-eight
veintinueve	twenty-nine
treinta	thirty
cuarenta	forty
cincuenta	fifty
sesenta	sixty
setenta	seventy
ochenta	eighty
noventa	ninety
cien(to)	one hundred
mil	one thousand

From the thirties through the nineties units are expressed by simply adding *y* and the numbers uno to nueve.

treinta y uno	thirty-one
sesenta y dos	sixty-two

VOCABULARIO

A

abandonar	to abandon
abogado [el]	lawyer
abuelo [el]	grandfather
abuela [la]	grandmother
acción [la]	stock
acusar	to charge, acknowledge
acerca de	about
afición [la]	hobby
agente [el]	agent, officer
agente encargado de la libertad provisional	probation officer
agente de bienes raíces	real estate agent
agencia [la]	agency
agua [el]	water
agua caliente	hot water
ahora	now
ahorro [el]	savings
albergue	shelter
ajustarse	to adjust
alergia [la]	allergy
alguno [a]	any
algo	anything
allá	there
alimento [el]	food
el servicio de alimentos	Meals on Wheels
alquilar	to rent
alquiler [el]	the rent
alto [a]	high
amante [el or la]	lover

amigo [el]	friend (male)
amiga [la]	friend (female)
anciano [el]	elderly person
andador [el]	walker
anormal	abnormal
anterior	former
antes	before
año [el]	year
aprobar	to approve
arreglar	to repair, arrange
arreglo [el]	arrangement
arreglos [los]	repairs
arrendamiento, contrato de	lease
arrestar	to arrest
aparato [el]	appliance
asistencia [la]	aid
asistir	to attend
asunto [el]	matter
atrasado	behind
ayudar	to help, aid

B

bajarse	to get off, get down from
bajo	low, below
en libertad provisional	on probation
en libertad bajo palabra	on parole
baño [el]	bathroom, restroom, bath
barrio [el]	neighborhood
bastón [el]	cane
basura [la]	garbage
bautismo [el]	baptism
bebida [la]	drink
beca [la]	scholarship
beneficios	benefits
bienes raíces	real estate

Bienestar Social	Welfare
bruto [en]	gross
bono [el]	bond
bueno	good
buscar	to look for

C

cabeza [la]	head (dolor de cabeza - headache)
calefacción [la]	heat
caliente	hot
cama [la]	bed
campo [el]	field
cantidad [la]	quantity (¿Qué cantidad? - How much?)
carácter [el]	character, behavior
cárcel [la]	jail
casa [la]	house
casarse	to get married
cita [la]	appointment
carro [el]	car
ciudadano [a]	citizen
clínica [la]	clinic
cobrar	to collect
¿cómo?	how?
cómodo [a]	comfortable
completar	to complete
comprar	to buy
comprender	to understand
conferencia del comité juvenil [la]	juvenile conference committee
cónyuge	spouse
consejo [el]	counselling
conocer	to know
consigo	with her, with him
contestar	to answer
contrato [el]	contract (-de arrendamiento - lease)

convenir	to be convenient
contento [a]	happy
corte [la]	court
¿cuándo?	when?
¿cuánto?	how much?
cucaracha [la]	cockroach
cuidado [el]	care
cuidar	to care for
cupón [el]	coupon

CH

cheque[el]	check
chinche [la]	bedbug

D

dar	to give
decir	to say
declarar	to declare
dejar	to leave
deletrear	to spell
demostrar	to show
dentista [el]	dentist
departamento [el]	department (-de Sanidad - Board of Health)
deprimido [a]	depressed
derecho	right
desalojar	to evict
desear	to wish
desempleo [el]	unemployment
deudas [las]	debts
día [el]	day
dinero [el]	money

dirección [la]	address
director de la escuela [el]	the school principal
distribuir	to distribute
divorciarse	to get a divorce
doblar	to turn
dolor [el]	pain, sorrow
¿dónde?	where?
dormir	sleep
dueño /el/	owner, landlord

E

económico	economic
edad [la]	age
elegibilidad [la]	eligibility
embarazo [el]	pregnancy
embarazada	pregnant
embargo [el]	lien
embolia [la]	stroke
emplear	to employ
enfermera [la]	nurse
entrevista [la]	interview
entrenamiento [el]	training
escuela [la]	school
escribir	to write
espalda [la]	back
esperar	to expect
espejuelos [los]	glasses
especialización [la]	specialty
esposo [el]	husband
esposa [la]	wife
esquina [la]	corner
estado civil [el]	marital status
Estados Unidos [los]	United States
estar	to be
estómago [el]	stomach
estudiar	study

estudios [los]	studies
explicar	to explain
exterminador [el]	exterminator

F

falta [la]	lack, loss
familia [la]	family
familiar	family member, relative
farmacia [la]	pharmacy
fecha [la]	date
forma [la]	way
formulario [el]	form
frecuencia	frequency
fuera de	outside of
fumar	to smoke

G

gimnasio [el]	gym, physical education
ginecólogo [el]	gynecologist
gremio [el]	union
gustar	to like

H

haber	to have (auxiliary verb)
habilidad [la]	skill
hablar	to talk
hacer	to do, to make
hija [la]	daughter

hijo [el]	son
hipoteca [la]	mortgage
hogar [el]	home
hombro	shoulder
hora /la/	time

I

impuesto [el]	tax
incapacidad [la]	disability
incluir	to include
indicar	to indicate
inglés [el]	English
ingresos [los]	profits
inscribirse	to enroll
insultarse	to insult
izquierda [la]	the left

L

lectura [la]	reading
libertad bajo palabra [la]	parole
libertad provisional [la]	probation
lugar [el]	place
luz [la]	light

LL

llamar	to call, phone
llamarse	to be named
llegar	to arrive, get (to a place)

M

madre	mother
maestro [el]	teacher (m.)
maestra [la]	teacher (f.)
malestar por la mañana [el]	morning sickness
manejar	to drive
mantenimiento [el]	maintenance, support
mantener	to maintain, support
mañana [la]	tomorrow, morning
matrimonial	marital
mayor	bigger, older
medicina [la]	medicine, medication
médico [el]	doctor, medical
medio	half
menor	less, younger
metro [el]	subway
miembro [el]	member
mientras	while
mismo [a]	same
modelo [el]	sample
momento [el]	moment (en este --- at present)
mudarse	to move
mujer [la]	woman, wife

N

nacer	to be born
nacimiento [el]	birth
necesitar	to need
nerviosismo [el]	nervousness
nieto [a]	grandchild
niñera	babysitter
niño [a]	child
noche [la]	evening, night

nombre [la]	name
nuestro [a]	our
número [el]	number

O

obedecer	to obey
obtener	obtain, get
ocuparse	to handle, be busy with
oficina [la]	office
optometrista [el]	optometrist
orden	order

P

pagar	to pay
pagos [los]	payments
padre [el]	father
padres [los]	parents
país [el]	country
palabra [la]	word
pared [la]	wall
parada de ómnibus [la]	bus stop
pariente [el]	relative
pasado [a]	past, last
patrono [el]	boss, employer
pedir	to request, ask for
pegar	to fight, beat up
pelea [la]	fight
pérdida [la]	loss
permiso [el]	permission (con permiso - excuse me)
pensar	to think, expect, contemplate
pertenecer	to belong

perro [el]	dog
petróleo [el]	oil
peso [el]	weight
piojo [el]	louse
piso [el]	floor, story
poder	can, to be able
ponerse	to become, make oneself
por favor	please
planeamiento [el]	planning
preferir	to prefer
pregunta [la]	question
preguntar	to ask
presentar	to present, to file (charges) to submit an application)
presión [la]	pressure
prima [la]	cousin (f.)
primo [el]	cousin (m.)
prisión [la]	prison
propio [a]	own
proveer	to provide
próximo [a]	next
pueblo [el]	town

Q

¿qué?	what?
que	that
quedarse	to stay
quejarse	to complain
querer	to wish, want, like to

R

ratón [el]	mouse, rat

razón [la]	reason
recibir	to receive
recibo [el]	receipt
recordar	to remember
reformatorio [el]	reformatory
relación [la]	relationship
relacionado [a]	related to, regarding
religioso [a]	religious
remitir	to refer

S

saber	to know
sacerdote [el]	priest
salud [la]	health
seguridad social [la]	social security
seguro [el]	insurance
senil	senile
sentarse	to sit down, be seated
separarse	to separate
ser	to be
servicio [el]	service
servicio de alimentos a domicilio	Meals on Wheels
silla de ruedas [la]	wheel chair
sobrina [la]	niece (sobrina nieta - grand-niece)
sobrino [el]	nephew (sobrino nieto - grand-nephew)
sobre	about, concerning
social	social
solamente	only
solitario [a]	lonely, alone
sótano [el]	basement
subterráneo [el]	subway
suceder	to happen
sueño [el]	sleep

T

tarde	late
tarde [la]	afternoon
taxi [el]	taxi
techo [el]	roof
teléfono [el]	telephone
temer	to be afraid of
tener	to have
tía [la]	aunt
tío [el]	uncle
tiempo [el]	time, weather (¿Por cuánto tiempo? - How long?)
trabajador [el]	worker (m.)
trabajadora [la]	worker (f.)
trabajo [el]	work
transporte [el]	transportation
tren [el]	train
todo [a]	all, every
tomar	to take, drink

U

úlcera [la]	ulcer
últimamente	lately
último [a]	late, last
usar	to use
usted /Ud./	you (sing.)
ustedes /Uds./	you (plural)

V

vacuna [la]	innoculation
valor [el]	value

vecina [la]	neighbor (f.)
vecino [el]	neighbor (m.)
vender	to sell
venir	to come
venta [la]	sale
ventana [la	window
verificar	to verify, check
veterano [el]	veteran
visitar	to visit
vivac [el]	house of detention (el vivac del condado - county home)
vivienda [la]	housing
vivir	to live

VOCABULARIO

A

abandon	abandonar
abnormal	anormal
about	acerca de
about *[concerning]*	sobre
accuse *[to]*	acusar
address	dirección (la)
adjust	ajustarse
afraid	temer
afternoon	tarde (la)
age	edad (la)
agency	agencia (la)
agent *[(officer]*	agente (el)
aid	asistencia (la)
all	todo
allergy	alergia (la)
alone	solitario (a)
answer *[to]*	contestar
any	alguno (a)
anything	algo
appliance	aparato (el)
appointment	cita (a)
approve	aprobar
arrange *[to]*	arreglar
arrangement	arreglo (el)
arrest *[to]*	arrestar
arrive *[to]*	llegar
ask for *[to]*	pedir
ask *[to]*	preguntar
attend *[to]*	asistir
aunt	tía (la)

B

babysitter	niñera (la)

back	espalda (la)
baptism	bautismo (el)
basement	sótano (el)
bath	baño (el)
bathroom	cuarto de baño (el)
be /to/	estar
be /to/	ser
become /to/	ponerse
bed	cama (la)
bedbug	chinche (la)
before	antes
behind	atrasado
belong /to/	pertenecer
below	bajo
benefits	beneficios
birth	nacimiento (el)
Board of Health	Departamento (el) de Sanidad
bond	bono (el)
born, to be	nacer
boss	patrono (el)
bus stop	parada de ómnibus (la)
busy	ocupado
buy	comprar

C

call /to/	llamar
cane	bastón (el)
can	poder
car	carro (el)
care	cuidado (el)
care for /to/	cuidar
character	carácter (el)
charge /to/	acusar
check	cheque (el)
child	niño (a)
citizen	ciudadano (a)
clinic	clínica (la)
cockroach	cucaracha (la)
collect /to/	cobrar

come *[to]*	venir
comfortable	cómodo (a)
complain *[to]*	quejarse
complete*[to]*	completar
contract	contrato (el)
convenient	convenir, conveniente
corner	esquina (la)
counselling	consejo (el)
county home	vivac (el)
country	país (el)
coupon	cupón (el)
court	corte (la)
cousin *[f.]*	prima (la)
cousin *[m.]*	primo (el)

D

date	fecha (la)
daughter	hija (la)
day	día (el)
debts	deudas (las)
declare *[to]*	declarar
dentist	dentista (el)
department	departamento (el)
depressed	deprimido (a)
disability	incapacidad (la)
distribute *[to]*	distribuir
do *[to]*	hacer
doctor	médico (el)
dog	perro (el)
drink *[to]*	tomar, beber

E

economic	económico
elderly person	anciano (el)
eligibility	elegibilidad (la)
employ *[to]*	emplear
English	inglés (el)

enroll	inscribirse
evening	noche (la)
every	todo (a)
evict /to/	desalojar
expect /to/	esperar
explain /to/	explicar
exterminator	exterminador (el)

F

family	familia (la)
family member	familiar, pariente
father	padre (el)
field	campo (el)
fight	pelea (la)
fight /beat up/ /to/	pegar
floor	piso (el)
food	alimento (el)
form	formulario (el)
former	anterior
frequency	frecuencia
friend /female/	amiga (la)
friend /male/	amigo (el)

G

garbage	basura (la)
get a divorce /to/	divorciarse
get married /to/	casarse
get off, get down from /to/	bajarse
get to a place /to/	llegar
give /to/	dar
glasses	espejuelos (los)
good	bueno
granchild	nieto (a)
grandfather	abuelo
grandmother	abuela
gross	bruto (en)
gym	gimnasio (el)

gynecologist	ginecólogo (el)

H

half	medio
happen /to/	suceder
happy	contento (a)
have /to/	haber, tener
head	cabeza (la)
headache	dolor de cabeza (el)
health	salud (la)
heat	calefacción (la)
help /to/	ayudar
high	alto (a)
hobby	afición (la)
home	hogar (el)
hot	caliente
hot water	agua caliente
house	casa (la)
house of detention	vivac (el)
housing	vivienda (la)
how?	¿cómo?
how much?	¿cuánto?
husband	esposo (el)

I

include /to/	incluir
indicate /to/	indicar
innoculation	vacuna (la)
insult /to/	insultar
insurance	seguro (el)
interview	entrevista (la)

J

jail	cárcel (la)

juvenile conference committee	conferencia del comité juvenil (la)

K

know *[to]*	conocer (to be acquainted with)
	saber (to have knowledge)

L

lack	falta (la)
landlord	dueño (el)
last	último (a)
late	tarde
lately	últimamente
lawyer	abogado (el)
lease	arrendamiento, contrato
leave *[to]*	dejar
left *[the]*	izquierda
less	menor, menos
lien	embargo (el)
light	luz (la)
like (to)	gustar
live *[to]*	vivir
look for *[to]*	buscar
loss	pérdida (la)
louse	piojo (el)
lover	amante (el or la)
low	bajo

M

maintain, support *[to]*	mantener
maintenance	mantenimiento (el)
make *[to]*	hacer
marital	matrimonial

marital status	estado civil (el)
matter	asunto (el)
Meals on Wheels	el servicio de alimentos
medicine	medicina (la)
member	miembro (el)
moment	momento (el)
money	dinero (el)
morning sickness	malestar por la mañana (el)
mortgage	hipoteca (la)
mother	madre (la)
mouse	ratón (el)
move *[to]*	mudarse

N

name	nombre (el)
named *[to be]*	llamarse
need *[to]*	necesitar
neighbor *[f.]*	vecina (la)
neighbor *[m.]*	vecino (el)
neighborhood	barrio (el)
nephew	sobrino (el)
nervousness	nerviosismo (el)
next	próximo (el)
niece	sobrina (la)
night	noche (la)
now	ahora
number	número (el)
nurse	enfermera (la)

O

obey *[to]*	obedecer
obtain *[to]*	obtener
office	oficina (la)
oil	petróleo (el)

only	solamente
optometrist	optometrista (el)
order	ordenar
our	nuestro (a)
outside of	fuera de
own	propio (a)
owner	dueño (el)

P

pain	dolor (el), pena (la)
parents	padres (los)
parole	libertad bajo palabra (la)
parole /to/	en libertad bajo palabra
past	pasado (a)
pay /to/	pagar
pay, to collect	pagar, recaudar
payments	pagos (los)
permission	permiso (el)
pharmacy	farmacia (la)
phone /to/	llamar por teléfono
physical education	gimnasia (la)
place	lugar (el)
planning	planeamiento (el)
please	por favor
prefer /to/	preferir
pregnancy	embarazo (el)
pregnant	embarazada
present /to/	presentar
pressure	presión (la)
priest	sacerdote (el)
prison	prisión (la)
probation /on/	en libertad provisional
probation officer	agente encargado de la libertad
profits	ingresos (los)
provide /to/	proveer

Q

quantity	cantidad
question	pregunta (la)

R

reading	lectura (la)
real estate	bienes raíces
real estate agent	agente de bienes raíces
reason	razón (la)
receipt	recibo (el)
receive /to/	recibir
refer /to/	remitir
reformatory	reformatorio (el)
related to	relacionado (a)
relationship	relación (la)
relative	pariente (el)
religious	religioso (a)
remember /to/	recordar
rent /the/	alquiler (el)
rent /to/	alquilar
repair /to/	arreglar
repairs	arreglos (los)
right	derecho
roof	techo (el)

S

sale	venta (la)
same	mismo (a)
sample	modelo (el)
savings	ahorro (el)
say /to/	decir
scholarship	beca (la)
school	escuela (la)
school principal	director de la escuela (el)
sell /to/	vender
senile	senil

separate /to/	separarse
service	servicio (el)
shelter	albergue
shoulder	hombro (el)
show /to/	demostrar
sit down /to/	sentarse
skill	habilidad (la)
sleep /to/	dormir
smoke /to/	fumar
social	social
Social Security	seguridad social (la)
son	hijo (el)
sorrow	dolor (el pena (la)
specialty	especialización (la)
spell /to/	deletrear
spouse	cónyuge
stay /to/	quedarse
stock	acción (la)
stomach	estómago (el)
stroke	embolia (la)
studies	estudios (los)
study /to/	estudiar
subway	subterráneo (el), metro (el)

T

take, drink /to/	tomar
talk /to/	hablar
tax	impuesto (el)
taxi	taxi (el)
teacher /f./	maestra (la)
teacher /m./	maestro (el)
telephone	teléfono (el)
that	que
there	allá
think /to/	pensar
time	hora (la)
	tiempo (el)
tomorrow	mañana
town	pueblo (el)
train	tren (el)

training	entrenamiento (el)
transportation	transporte (el)
turn /to/	doblar

U

ulcer	úlcera (la)
uncle	tío (el)
understand /to/	comprender
unemployment	desempleo (el)
union	gremio (el)
United States	Estados Unidos (los)
use /to/	usar

V

value	valor (el)
verify /to/	verificar
veteran	veterano (el)
visit /to/	visitar

W

walker	andador (el)
wall	pared (la)
want /to/	querer
water	agua (el)
way /the manner/	forma (la)
weather	tiempo (el)
weight	peso (el)
Welfare	Bienestar Social
what?	¿qué?
wheel chair	silla de ruedas (la)
when?	¿cuándo?
where?	¿dónde?
while	mientras
wife	esposa (la)

window	ventana (la)
wish *[to]*	desear
with him/her	consigo
woman	mujer (la)
word	palabra (la)
work	trabajo (el)
worker *[f.]*	trabajadora (la)
worker *[m.]*	trabajador (el)
write *[to]*	escribir

Y

year	año (el)
you *[sing.]*	usted (Ud.)
you *[plural]*	ustedes (Uds.)
younger	menor

INDEX

Preface 7

Introduction 9

Pronunciation 13

Punctuation 15

Grammar Notes 17

Worker-Client Communication 19

Forms 42

Spanish Verbs and Subject Pronouns 63

Regular Verbs 64

Irregular Verbs 66

Cardinal Numbers 69

Vocabulario español-inglés 71

Vocabulary English-Spanish 84